HOPSCOTCH
STORIES OF
RELIGION

The
Flight from
Makkah

First published in 2009 by
Franklin Watts
338 Euston Road
London
NW1 3BH

Franklin Watts Australia
Level 17/207 Kent Street
Sydney
NSW 2000

A CIP catalogue record for this book is available
from the British Library.

ISBN 978 0 7496 8373 3 (hbk)
ISBN 978 0 7496 8379 5 (pbk)

Series Editor: Melanie Palmer
Series Advisor: Dr Barrie Wade
Series Designer: Peter Scoulding
Consultant: Professor Ghulam Sarwar

Printed in China

Franklin Watts is a division of
Hachette Children's Books,
an Hachette Livre UK company
www.hachettelivre.co.uk

The
Flight from
Makkah

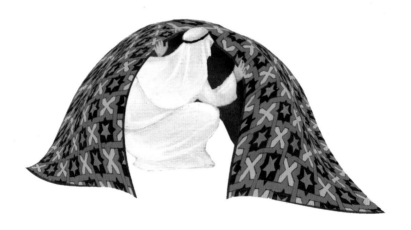

by Anita Ganeri and Serena Curmi

W
FRANKLIN WATTS
LONDON•SYDNEY

About this book

The story of the Flight from Makkah comes from the religion of Islam. Islam began in the Middle East about 1,400 years ago. Muslims (followers of Islam) believe that Allah (God) sent a series of prophets to teach people how to live. The last and greatest of these was Muhammad (Peace Be Upon Him*). Muhammad (PBUH) was born in the city of Makkah in Arabia (modern-day Saudi Arabia) in about 570 CE. *The Flight from Makkah* tells how he escaped from people plotting his death and fled to Madinah in 622 CE. His journey is known as the *hijrah* (flight).

* This is abbreviated to PBUH after the first mention. Following Islamic tradition, the illustrations in this book do not show faces of people or depictions of Allah or Muhammad (PBUH).

For many years, the Prophet
Muhammad (Peace Be Upon Him)
lived in the city of Makkah.

Muhammad (PBUH) taught people about Allah, and many people became Muslims like him.

But the rich merchants of Makkah were afraid of losing their power if people worshipped Allah.

Allah told Muhammad (PBUH) to leave Makkah and travel to the city of Madinah.

The merchants were plotting to kill Muhammad (PBUH). They did not want him in their city.

The angel Jibril warned
Muhammad (PBUH) about
the merchants' wicked plan.

So Muhammad's (PBUH) cousin,
Ali, slept in Muhammad's (PBUH)
bed instead. The merchants were
furious when they found out.

Meanwhile, Muhammad (PBUH) and his friend Abu Bakr quickly escaped.

They set off on two camels,
on the long journey across
the desert to Madinah.

Muhammad (PBUH) and his friend Abu rode fast, but the merchants were not far behind them.

Just then Muhammad (PBUH) and Abu saw a cave. They knew that Allah would keep them safe there.

From the cave, they heard the merchants. Their voices got louder as they rode nearer.

"Over there! A cave!" said one merchant. "Maybe they're hiding inside it. Let's look!"

"'No one's been here for years," said another merchant. "Look, the entrance is covered with cobwebs."

18

The merchants could not find Muhammad (PBUH) so they gave up their search and went home.

Inside the cave, Muhammad (PBUH) and Abu Bakr were filled with relief. They were safe at last.

"Where did those cobwebs come from?" asked Abu Bakr. "They weren't there before."

Muhammad (PBUH) smiled at his friend. He knew that Allah had been watching over them.

The two men stayed in the cave for a while to make sure that they were safe.

Then they set off once more across the desert sands on their long and thirsty journey.

They rode all through the night, when it was cooler, and rested during the heat of the day.

News of Muhammad's (PBUH) journey from Makkah had already reached the people of Madinah.

Every day, they went to the edge
of the city and waited eagerly
for him to arrive.

At last, Muhammad (PBUH) and Abu Bakr reached Madinah. They were given a great welcome.

Many people invited Muhammad (PBUH) to stay in their houses. But the Prophet waited until his camel stopped to decide where to stay.

Finally, his camel rested near the house of Abu Ayyub Ansari. Muhammad (PBUH) stayed in the house for a few days.

Then he built a mosque and a house to live in, and brought great joy to the people of Madinah.

Hopscotch has been specially designed to fit the requirements of the Literacy Framework. It offers real books by top authors and illustrators for children developing their reading skills.

For more details go to:
www.franklinwatts.co.uk

* hardback